SAE EDGE™
RESEARCH REPORT

Unsettled Topics on the Feasibility and Desirability of Using Additive Manufacturing in the Mobility Industry

Kevin T. Slattery, DSc
The Barnes Group Advisors

EDGE DEVELOPMENT TEAM

Christopher Aldridge, *The Barnes Group Advisors*
David Dietrich, PhD, *Honeywell*
Jerry Halley, *Tech Manufacturing*
Ron Daul, *General Motors*
Anthony Rollett, PhD, *Carnegie Mellon University*
Jennifer Coyne, *Wabtec*

SAE INTERNATIONAL®

Warrendale, Pennsylvania, USA

About the Publisher

SAE International® is a global association of more than 128,000 engineers and related technical experts in the aerospace, automotive, and commercial-vehicle industries. Our core competencies are lifelong learning and voluntary consensus standards development. Visit sae.org

SAE EDGE™ Research Report Disclaimer

SAE EDGE™ Research Reports focus on topics that are dynamic, in which knowledge is incomplete, and which have yet to be standardized. They represent the collective wisdom of a group of experts and serve as a practical guide to the reader in understanding unsettled subject matter. They are not meant to provide a recommended practice or protocol. The experts have assembled as a community of practitioners to contribute and collectivize their thoughts and points of view; these are not the positions of the institutions or businesses with which they are affiliated nor is one contributor's perspective advanced over other contributors. SAE EDGE™ Research Reports are the property of SAE International, and SAE alone is responsible for their content.

About This Publication

SAE EDGE™ Research Reports provide state-of-the-art and state-of-the-industry examinations of the most significant topics in mobility engineering. SAE EDGE™ contributors are experts from research, academia, and industry who have come together to explore and define the most critical advancements, challenges, and future direction in areas such as vehicle automation, unmanned aircraft, cybersecurity, advanced propulsion, advanced manufacturing, Internet of Things, and connectivity.

Related Resources

SAE MOBILUS® Advanced Manufacturing Hub
https://saemobilus.sae.org/advanced-manufacturing/

SAE Team

Frank Menchaca, Chief Product Officer
Michael Thompson, Director, Standards, Information, and Research Publications
Monica Nogueira, Acquisitions Director
Beth Ellen Dibeler, Product Manager
William Kucinski, Managing Technical Editor

Printed in USA

EPR2020009
ISSN 2640-3536
e-ISSN 2640-3544
ISBN 978-1-4686-0171-8

To purchase bulk quantities, please contact: SAE Customer Service

E-mail: CustomerService@sae.org
Phone: 877-606-7323 (*inside USA and Canada*)
+1-724-776-4970 (*outside USA*)
Fax: +1-724-776-0790

https://www.sae.org/publications/edge-research-reports

About the Editor

Kevin T. Slattery, DSc - Kevin is a Principal ADDvisor® at The Barnes Group Advisors. His primary expertise is in Metallic Additive and Metals Manufacturing, focusing on test program development, process and product verification, qualification, and certification. He has supported over 25 clients on five continents throughout the entire additive manufacturing value chain from raw material to finished components.

Kevin was previously the Chief Scientist for Additive Manufacturing at Boeing Research and Technology (BR&T). He was responsible for developing and integrating the technical roadmaps and development plans for metallic additive manufacturing for the entire company, along with building and leading a multi-skilled team to execute and deliver the technology throughout the enterprise. Prior to that, he was the Chief Scientist for Metals, Ceramics, and Mechanical Systems at BR&T, with the responsibility for portfolio development and coordination, while executing the additive manufacturing portion.

He served as the Division Chief Engineer for the U.S. Navy and U.S. Air Force fighter aircraft and U.S. Army rotorcraft in Boeing's Military Sustainment organization. From 1997 to 2012, he was on the BR&T Metals Team as a researcher and senior manager, where he primarily developed advanced low-cost titanium-processing technologies supporting all Boeing products. He was the technical and programmatic lead in implementing the first aerospace metal additive-manufactured structural aircraft components for both spares and production, along with five other first-in-industry technology implementations.

He began his career at McDonnell Douglas (now Boeing) as a nondestructive testing engineer, where he developed inspection technologies for metallic and composite components, along with integrating the impact of discontinuities with the acceptance criteria for carbon/epoxy composites.

Dr. Slattery holds BS and MS degrees in Metallurgical Engineering from the University of Missouri-Rolla (now Missouri S&T) and a DSc in Material Science and Engineering from Washington University in St. Louis. He currently holds 36 U.S. patents, with another 15 applications pending, along with 36 significant publications and conference presentations.

contents

Atosan/Shutterstock.com

Unsettled Topics on the Feasibility and Desirability of Using Additive Manufacturing in the Mobility Industry

Abstract

Depending on the industry and application, views on additive manufacturing (AM), or "3D printing," range from something that will transform an industry to it being another overhyped technology that will only find niche applications. Most views fall somewhere in between, with the most common one being that it depends on the application and technology. Because of the ability to directly produce parts from a digital file, views often include dependence on when and where the part is needed. This introduces the crux of the matter, which is how to determine when the use of AM is feasible and desirable, which is made all the more complicated by the fact that not only is AM technology in general changing quickly, but also the merits of the each AM technology relative to the others are also changing. Finally, non-AM technologies are continually improving and are increasingly adding AM-like capability.

As the opening report of a six-part series of SAE EDGE™ Research Reports on AM, this paper discusses unsettled issues pertaining to the benefits, drawbacks, and trade-offs, as well as the decision-making processes to be followed in determining the feasibility and desirability of using AM.

NOTE: SAE EDGE™ Research Reports are intended to identify and illuminate key issues in emerging, but still unsettled, technologies of interest to the mobility industry. The goal of SAE EDGE™ Research Reports is to stimulate discussion and work in the hope of promoting and speeding resolution of identified issues. SAE EDGE™ Research Reports are not intended to resolve the challenges they identify or close any topic to further scrutiny.

Regarding terminology

- System refers to an end product that serves a unique role to the user (aircraft, automobile, etc.).
- Part refers to an individual component that cannot be taken apart without destroying it (machinings, stampings, weldments, etc.).
- Subsystem refers to a distinct collection of parts within a system (braking, actuation, etc.) or structure (trunk lid, flap, etc.) that have a defined role.
- Subassembly refers to a collection of parts, or a series of parts unitized together, that performs a defined role in a subsystem.

KEVIN T. SLATTERY, DSc
The Barnes Group Advisors

Edge Development Team

Christopher Aldridge, *The Barnes Group Advisors*
David Dietrich, PhD, *Honeywell*
Jerry Halley, *Tech Manufacturing*
Ron Daul, *General Motors*
Anthony Rollett, PhD, *Carnegie Mellon University*
Jennifer Coyne, *Wabtec*

ISSN 2640-3536

Introduction

The State of Additive Manufacturing in the Mobility Industry

The transition of additive manufacturing (AM), or "3D printing," over the last 30 years - from a method to rapidly make prototypes with only dimensional requirements to one that produces performance-critical parts by the thousands for a variety of industries - illustrates how dramatically lasers (in most cases) and increased computing power have transformed life in the twenty-first century. Now that AM has become the primary method of manufacturing in some cases, such as custom hearing aids, it makes sense to ask why it has made such limited impact in others. How can one determine when AM makes sense for a given part, system, and industry? Also, as both AM and competing technologies continue to evolve, when is it feasible and desirable to use AM versus other technologies, and which AM technology is the most appropriate? As a result of this continuing evolution, the feasibility and desirability of using AM to make a part or subsystem represents an unsettled topic in transportation.

The first consideration in the use of any manufacturing technology is whether the process can produce a part or combination of parts that reliably meets service requirements. In other words, is it feasible to make the desired part or subsystem? Determining feasibility in the case of AM is not simple, as the range of AM already covers seven different process categories as defined by the ASTM F42 committee. There are multiple processes under each category, each of which has different available materials, size ranges, and geometric capabilities. Table 1 illustrates the broad range of different processes and their variants. While every material/feedstock/energy source/post-processing combination is not currently utilized, many of them exist, with each having its advantages and disadvantages for a given application.

A basic determination of feasibility is whether or not AM can produce a part in a material and size that meets engineering requirements. The second determination regards designing around the limitations of the candidate AM processes. While we are used to hearing how AM opens new design space, and complexity is free; like any other manufacturing process, each AM process comes with its own constraints. Thus feasibility needs to address the ability of the candidate AM processes to build a part without undue performance limitations, such as additional weight, thermal gradients, and inspectability and reliability issues. Once feasibility is addressed, the desirability of using AM can be determined.

The actual application for the part or subsystem under consideration plays a large role in determining the desirability of using AM. Each application type contains a broad range of considerations, or attributes, that each contribute to the determining the desirability of using AM:

- Feasibility/maturity of AM processes and materials
- Ability of AM to impact the performance of a part or subsystem

TABLE 1. Process categories and variants according to ASTM F42.

F42 Process	Material Systems	Feedstocks	Energy Sources	Post-Printing
Vat Photopolymerization	Polymer Ceramic	Liquid Ceramic in Liquid	Laser Radiant	Thermal Final Cure
Sheet Lamination	Organic Metal	Paper Sheets	Heat Conduction Ultrasonic	Stress Relief Autoclave Diffusion Bonding
Material Extrusion	Polymer Metal	Filament Rod, Powder	Heat Conduction Frictional Heating	Stress Relief Heat Treatment
Material Jetting	Polymer Metal Ceramic	Powder	Heat Conduction Radiant Heating	Debinding Sinter to Full Density
Binder Jet Printing	Polymer Metal Ceramic	Powder	Heat Convection Radiant Heating	Debinding Sinter to Full Density
Directed-Energy Deposition	Metal	Powder Wire	Arc/Plasma Laser Electron Beam Electric Resistance	Stress Relief Heat Treatment
Powder Bed Fusion	Polymer Metal	Powder	Laser Electron Beam	Stress Relief Heat Treatment

- Stability of the design of the part or subsystem
- Desired production quantities, production rate, and time span of production
- Lead time for the first part and subsequent parts
- Cost to produce the first part (including nonrecurring design and qualification) and subsequent parts
- Need to obtain replacement parts or repair worn parts to maintain system in service

The relative importance of each of these attributes can be used to determine the desirability of an AM application. Further complicating this is the evolving nature of AM technology, which means next year's answer may be different from today's answer. Also, the result can change while AM or another technology is in the process of being implemented or in production. While this can be driven by changes in requirements, design, or AM technology, it can also be influenced by changes in competing, generally conventional, manufacturing technologies.

While advancements in AM have garnered much attention over the last decade, the same advancements in computing and materials processing have led to conventional manufacturing technologies continually improving. This includes manufacturing technologies such as casting, machining, sheet metal forming, injection molding, and powder metallurgy. Some of these changes are making conventional manufacturing obtain more AM-like attributes, such as unitization and reduced nonrecurring costs. As a result, comparing today's AM technology with yesterday's conventional technology can often be invalid and result in higher costs and risks. Thus in determining the desirability of AM, a comparison of the trade-offs with current conventional technology must be made.

The mobility industry is pursuing AM to improve safety, to reduce cost (both purchase and operational) to their customers, and to get them new or improved products quicker. Many other technologies are being used in pursuit of the same three goals. Because AM is a new and rapidly evolving technology, the feasibility and desirability of using it in the mobility industry is unsettled. This SAE EDGE™ Research Report will describe the unsettled nature in the following four domains:

- Material and process selection
- Rationale for using AM
- Trade-offs in product design, development, and deployment
- Competing technologies

While a number of industries and product teams have come up with methods of determining the feasibility and desirability of using AM, many of these are either proprietary to the organization or specialized in their application, making this an unsettled topic of industry in general. This SAE EDGE™ Research Report will provide a framework for making such a determination to allow the user to devise their own methods to apply to their unique circumstances.

Material and Process Selection

Product Requirements

While the range of AM processes and material systems in Table 1 may appear broad, it is currently quite narrow when compared to conventional processes, which may have tens of polymers or hundreds of alloys for a designer to choose from. Additionally, each AM process has its own geometric capabilities and limitations to consider. This combination has led most organizations to come to the conclusion that a part needs to be designed with AM in mind for it to be a successful AM application. This practice is generally known as Design for Additive Manufacturing (DfAM).

Finally, like any other design-and-build activity, the requirements of the part and the capabilities of the process and material need to be considered in unison for a successful implementation. Thus the wide range of processes coupled with the limited, but growing, number of materials for each process and variant makes material and process selection unsettled in the feasibility and desirability of using AM. While this SAE EDGE™ Research Report is not intended to be an exhaustive review of the different AM materials and processes, the unsettled nature will be discussed using the seven ASTM F42 processes as an outline.

Vat Photopolymerization

Vat photopolymerization was the first "rapid prototyping" technology, as AM was then known, that many encountered. The process, shown in Figure 1, scans a light source, generally a laser, across the surface of a vat containing a liquid photopolymer. The light causes polymerization, turning a thin liquid layer into a solid. As the stage drops between layers, the curing polymer also bonds to the previous layer, creating a part. Post-processing can include a final thermal cure. Newer versions of the technology draw the part from the vat, with the light provided from below.

Because of the low mechanical properties of the photopolymers, and their moisture affinity, the process was generally used to illustrate concepts and for dimensional prototypes, with some use in wind tunnel models. It was also used in one of the first versions of indirect AM, known as QuickCast®, shown in Figure 2, where the part was used as a pattern for a ceramic investment casting mold. This avoided having to make an expensive and time-consuming metal mold during pre-production of a new investment casting. In this case, the relatively low mechanical properties were a benefit, as it prevented the pattern from stressing the ceramic mold during firing and pattern burnout.

While more recent versions of the technology have a greatly accelerated build rate, and materials with better mechanical properties are available, vat photopolymerization

FIGURE 1. **Vat photopolymerization.**

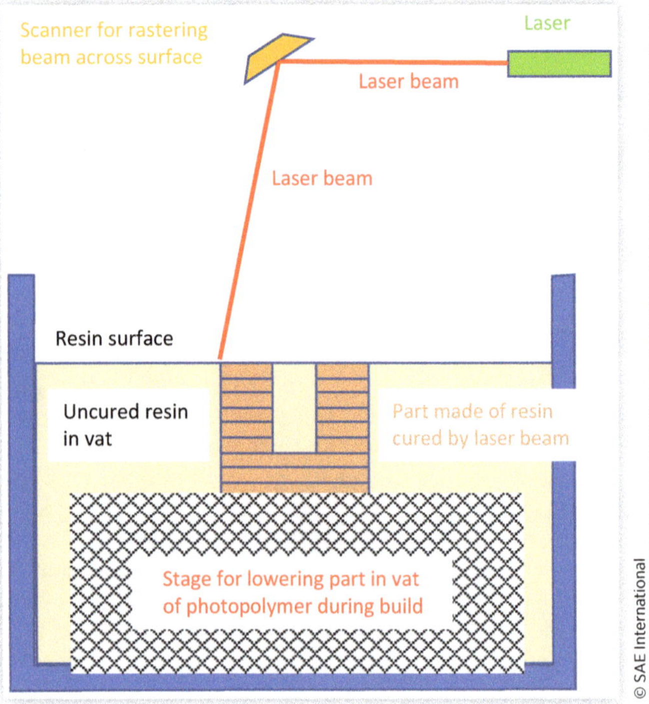

will, by definition, be restricted to a few materials, limiting it to a niche in the overall design space.

Material Extrusion

Since 2000, material extrusion is generally the first AM technology people encountered, as small polymer filament extrusion machines have become ubiquitous in schools and businesses of all types. The most common version of the process, shown in Figure 3, pushes a thermoplastic polymer filament through a heated tip that melts and fuses the filament to the previous and adjacent layers. Polymer variants of the technology can use multiple filaments of different colors or polymers, with one of the different materials used for any needed support structure. Polymer matrix composites have also been recently introduced. Another variant uses a filament, which is a mixture of polymer and metal, where the polymer is chemically or thermally removed and the remaining metal sintered at a high temperature; thus, metal parts at near full-density are produced. A final metal variant uses friction to heat and soften a metal rod or granules prior to extrusion.

Despite relatively low productivity compared to injection molding, which limits cost-effectiveness in high-volume applications, material extrusion leverages a wide range of polymeric materials (some with good impact resistance) and is relatively easy to use (as there are no liquid or powder print media). This has led to material extrusion becoming the dominant AM technology for producing tools, jigs, fixtures, and safety devices (ergonomic aids, protective covers, etc.) from polymers. This benefit also extends to low-rate production industries, such as aerospace, and spare parts production in higher rate industries. Newer metal and polymer matrix composite systems are considered to do the same where higher mechanical or thermal properties are needed.

Sheet Lamination

Unlike the previous two processes, sheet lamination has not been widely encountered in the mobility industry, not counting lamination of polymer matrix composites. That said, sheet lamination is one of the oldest AM processes, with an early version using adhesively backed heavy-duty paper to make prototypes and tooling (although moisture absorption often limited the use of the tool to short time periods) (Figure 4).

A newer version uses high-powered ultrasonic horns to laminate metal foils together. Because of the wide range of metal and polymer foils available, sheet lamination has great flexibility in material selection, including the ability to make parts from different metals and from metal/polymer laminates. However, unlike most other AM processes, sheet lamination requires a significant vertical force (usually referred to as Z-direction) during buildup. This tends to impose a bit of a geometric limitation to parts that are more 2D rather than 3D, and limits small cross-sectional features in the Z-direction. On the other hand, the lack of melting means that residual stresses and distortion are virtually nonexistent.

Powder Bed Fusion

Powder bed fusion (PBF) is the process that often comes to mind when people think of AM of metals, although it is widely used for thermoplastic polymers (neat and particulate reinforced) as well. While focused lasers are the most common energy source, an electron beam is also used for metals, with nonfocused lasers and infrared sources proposed for polymers and some low-melting-point metals (Figure 5). Thermoplastics and fusion weldable metals may be used, which provides a wide range of available materials. Because the process involves melting and solidification, thermal expansion and residual stresses are a significant consideration. This generally requires the part to be attached to a rigid build plate with supports during the build process, which are later removed after a stress-relief process. The use of melting and solidification also means that dramatic changes from layer to layer in terms of melt area or cross-section that need to be avoided. Thus, parts tend to be built in non-orthogonal directions, which can complicate design and analysis, and limit the size of a part that can be built in a chamber of a given size. The need for homogeneity, and because the majority of the powder that goes into the build chamber is recovered

FIGURE 2. **Indirect AM for investment casting.**

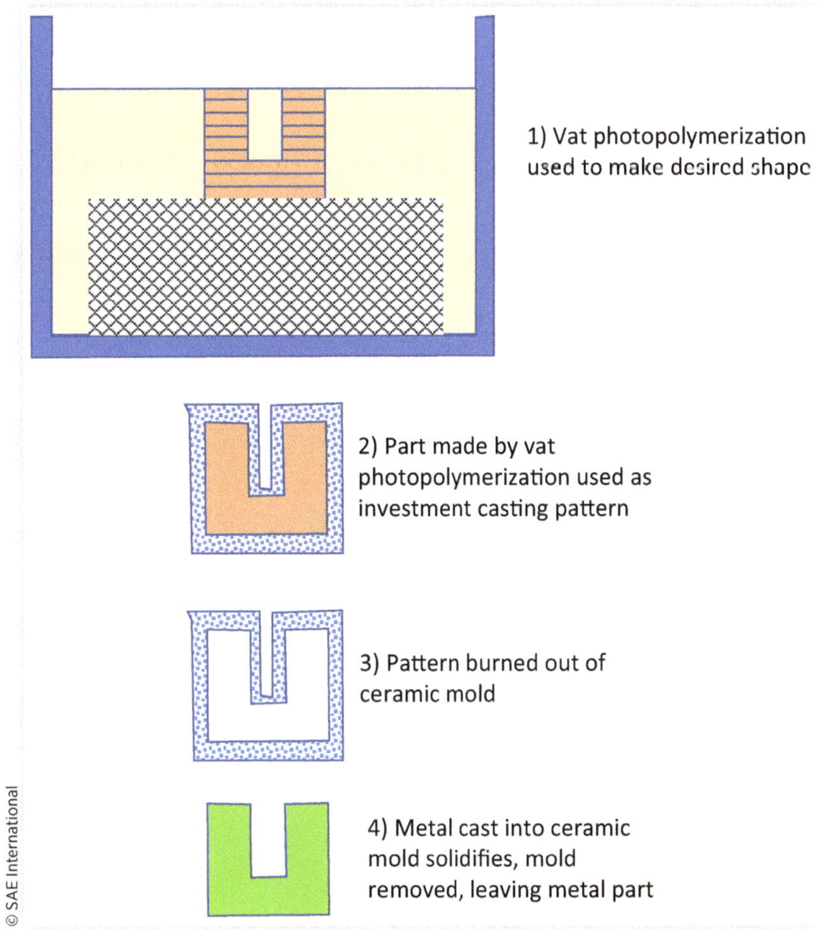

FIGURE 3. **Material extrusion.**

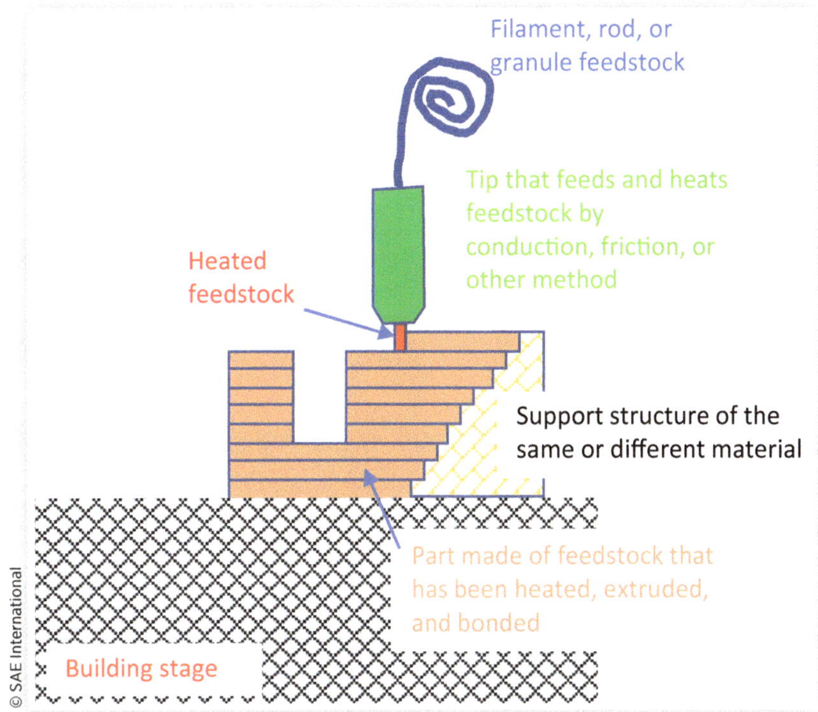

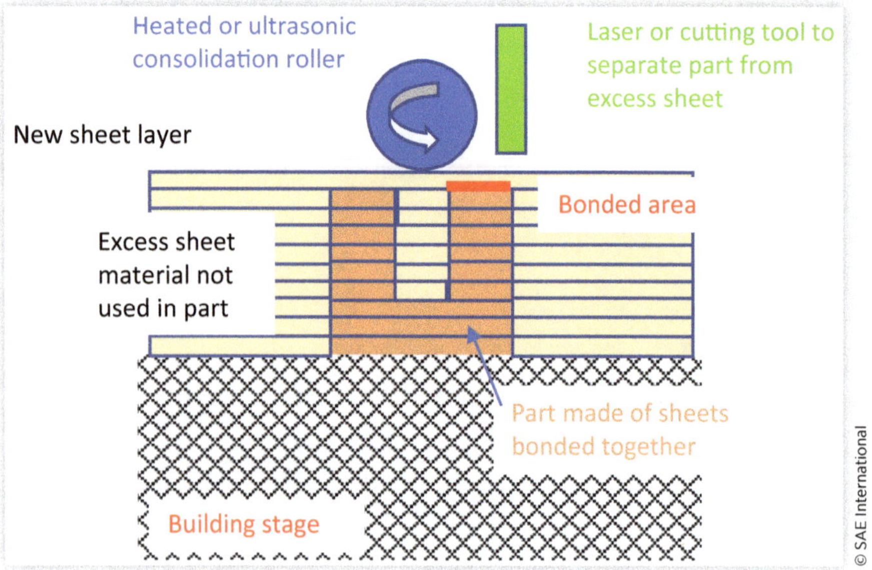

FIGURE 4. **Sheet lamination.**

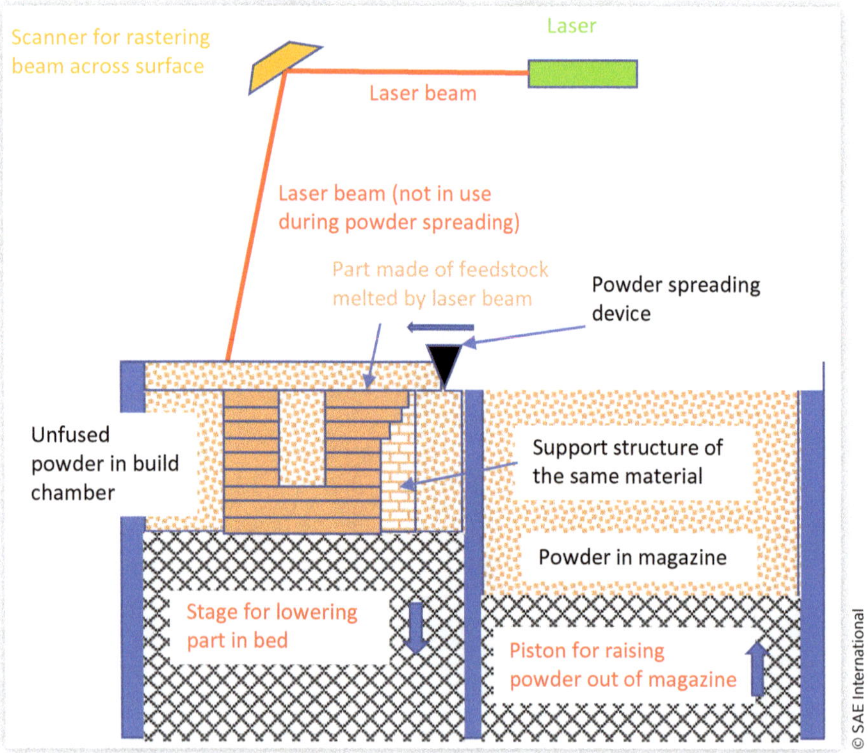

FIGURE 5. **PBF (laser version shown).**

and reused for future builds, means that almost all variants of the process use a single material for both the part and the supports.

PBF is the most widely known of the metal AM processes because of the demonstrated ability to make a complex part with features that conventional processing can rarely provide. This enables more efficient structural or fluid flow configurations. Primary limiting features are residual stress management, the need to ensure powder removal, and the rough surface (common to many AM processes) that can impact dimensions, fit-up, ability to undergo nondestructive testing (NDT), and fatigue loading.

Directed-Energy Deposition

Directed-energy deposition (DED) is the AM process that predates the use of the terms rapid prototyping and AM, which was known as weld buildup or buttering. As of this writing, DED is exclusive to metals in commercial use with the same requirement for fusion weldability (Figure 6). In general, DED is used for larger parts than PBF. In DED, the build plate is often made from the same alloy as the feedstock and becomes incorporated into the final part. Both wire and powder feedstocks are used with a wide range of energy sources, including arc, electron beam, laser, and electric resistance.

Some of the variants, generally with melt puddle sizes six millimeters and greater, are used to make a preform that is machined on 100% of the surfaces, including the base substrate. While this means that geometries are limited to those that can be machined, the rationale for using AM to make a fully machined structure is to reduce the amount of input stock (referred to as reducing the "buy-to-fly ratio" in aerospace) of high-cost materials such as titanium and nickel-based alloys, and thus reduce final part cost. There are other versions, referred to as hybrid manufacturing, that alternate deposition and machining passes to make parts that, while fully machined and which have reduced material consumption, can also have features not producible with conventional machining.

Depending on the number of machine axes, more or less support structure may be needed to make a part of complex geometry. Residual stress and distortion have to be managed, often more than in PBF due to the generally larger parts and puddle sizes.

Material Jetting

One of the newer AM processes, material jetting is the one that most resembles the term 3D printing in that much of the initial development used modified 2D inkjet printers (Figure 7). Because the process uses either liquid droplets or fine metal or ceramic powders in a liquid suspension, the range of materials and material combinations is the widest of all AM processes. Versions that use a stream of liquid-metal droplets are also being developed. This process is often used to make color-coded conceptual designs, as well as parts from elastomers and polymers. The use of droplets also provides a very high resolution, with the drawback being long build times and relatively small part sizes. Parts with metal and

FIGURE 6. Directed-Energy Deposition (DED).

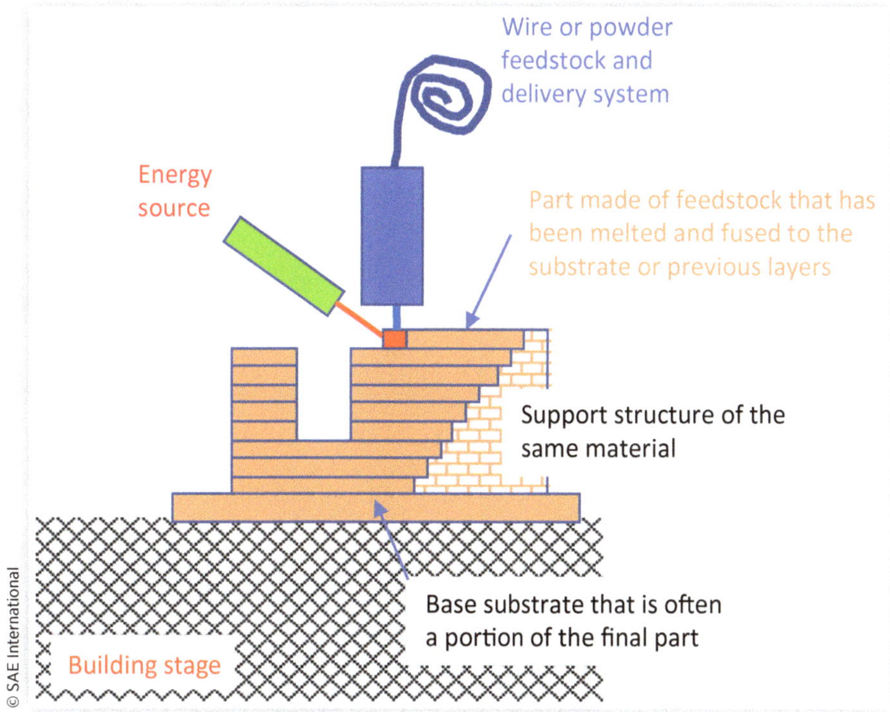

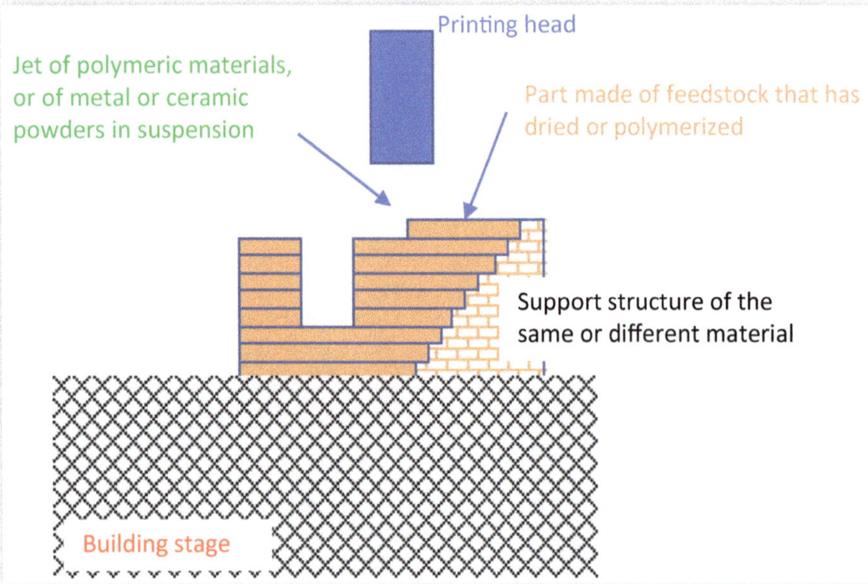

FIGURE 7. Material jetting.

ceramic powders can have the polymer removed (debinding) and sintered to near-full density, with the same resolution/size/build time trade-offs. Since nearly any material that is liquid or can be suspended in a liquid is potentially viable, there is significant interest in using material jetting to produce electronics or parts with unique physical properties.

Binder Jetting

As the one process that includes a post-processing step for completion, binder jetting can resemble a cross between PBF and material jetting (Figure 8). Both metal and ceramic powder sizes tend to run in between those of PBF and material jetting. While current commercial systems use either radiant or conductive heat for melting or rely on evaporation of a solvent liquid. The earliest versions of binder jetting used polymer laser PBF machines with a mixture of metal powder and polymers (powders or a coating on the metal particles) and used the laser to melt the polymer only to bind together the metal particles. Variants of this process can alternate spraying binder where the part is followed by spreading or dropping powder across the bed.

A widespread use of binder jetting is in indirect AM, where sand with a polymer binder is printed to make casting molds, which are then thermally processed to improve the strength of the mold. When used to directly make ceramic and powder metallurgy parts - after printing and removal from the powder bed - the parts (referred to as green parts) go through debinding (producing what is known as a brown part). The brown parts are then

- Sintered for a relatively short period of time to achieve enough strength to allow for infiltration with a second metal system

or

- Sintered to achieve near-full density

Because almost all metals and ceramics can be sintered, the range of materials is wider than for PBF, with some limitations on low-density systems with strong oxide coatings, such as aluminum and magnesium alloys. Essentially any material that can be processed with conventional powder metallurgy or metal injection molding technology is possible for binder jetting. This can include blended elemental powders which generally sinter more quickly and are sometimes cheaper. The primary geometric limitation on binder jetting is that the part must be able to be sintered, which can lead to limitations on unsupported overhangs (brown parts are very weak, especially at elevated temperatures) and overall size, as sagging of the overhangs or excessive friction on large parts can prevent attaining the needed dimensional tolerances.

Because binder jetting is a two-step process, the interaction between developing the printed green part and the sintered final part adds a level of complexity in process and product development. Parts with tight dimensional tolerances will require greater up-front effort. This is more challenging if there is anisotropy in the shrinkage behavior. One way to reduce the development time would be a designed experiment where a number of preforms with different dimensions are printed and sintered, providing part-specific relationships for the final green part design.

Recommendations

Because of the wide range of processes, the material and geometric limitations of each process, part requirements, material availability, and process capability must all be considered in unison when determining the feasibility

FIGURE 8. **Binder jetting.**

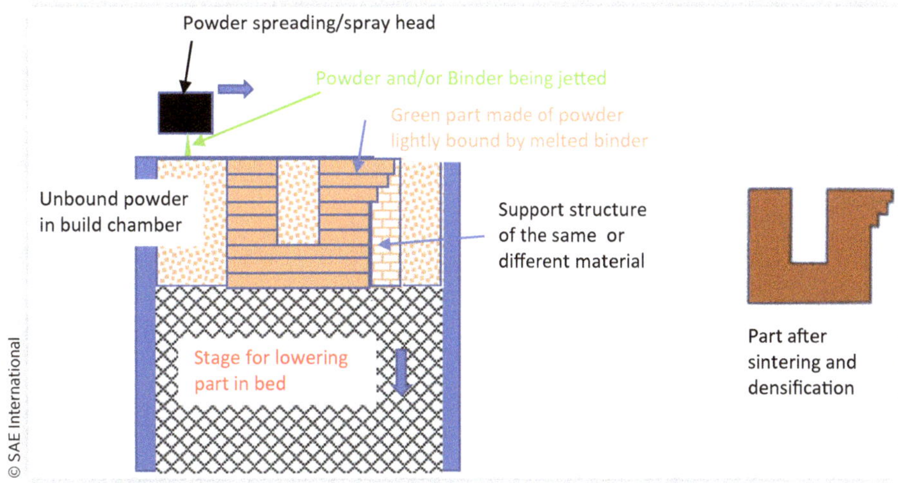

and desirability of using AM in the mobility industry. Further complicating decision-making is the continuous change in the technology with larger, faster, and more flexible machines becoming available on nearly a weekly basis. Finally, there is the challenge, not discussed in this report, of developing and qualifying the material, process, and part that provides a lag that can run from a few months to several years after introduction of a machine/material combination. All of this means that material and process selection are unresolved in looking to the horizon. Therefore, the recommendation for the design and manufacturing team looking for a beneficial implementation of AM is to look at when the final implementation needs to be successful, and determine the material and process combinations that provide a high probability of success in the desired time frame. This not only includes process and material maturity level but also considers the design trade space to include the entire range of materials and processes that can meet requirements.

Rationale for Using AM

Attributes for AM Selection

The selection of any manufacturing technology is dependent not only on the necessary part geometry and property requirements but also on the circumstances surrounding the need for the part in the first place (e.g., cost, lead time, service life, quantity). As AM encompasses a wide and rapidly evolving range of capabilities, the feasibility and desirability of using AM is dependent not only on the geometry and property requirements, but also on the circumstances surrounding the need at the time the part is committed to AM, and when the part is needed. Thus each potential application has a series of attributes that will influence the feasibility and desirability of using AM (Table 2).

To further illustrate these attributes, the following seven reasons will be used to demonstrate how the unsettled nature of evolving AM technologies can influence the feasibility and desirability of using AM in the mobility industry:

- Quicker and lower cost concepts and prototypes
- Quicker and lower cost tooling and safety devices
- Short-run spares, repairs, and hard-to-obtain/retain skills
- Cost reduction
- Mass customization
- Part-count reduction
- Performance improvements

In each one of these scenarios, an application type will be discussed, along with how the unsettled nature of AM technology can influence the feasibility and desirability of using AM in the mobility industry.

Quicker and Lower Cost Concepts and Prototypes

Progress and Unresolved Issues Since the AM industry developed out of technologies that were originally lumped under the category of rapid prototyping, this is the application area that is the most mature and has the fewest unresolved challenges. However, that was not the original case. Aerospace and automotive companies were among the first organizations to install vat photopolymerization machines in their model shops, taking advantage of the ability to quickly go from computer-aided design (CAD) to

TABLE 2. **Attributes in determining feasibility and desirability for using AM.**

Attribute	Description	Influence
Feasibility	• Can the process make a part of the desired size? • Can the process make a part of the desired geometry? • Can the process and material produce a part that meets service requirements?	• Generally negative. • If the answer to any of the questions is no, then the use of AM is not feasible, noting the use of indirect AM or a smaller AM part in an assembly may provide a different answer.
Part or Subsystem Performance Impact	• Can the feasible AM process and material combination result in a part or subsystem that has higher performance, such as lower weight, more compact size, more reliable, superior heat transfer?	• Varies directly with answer. • Most of the mobility industry values higher performance, which can be traded for negative influences like higher cost.
Part or Subsystem Design Stability	• Is the current design of the part or subsystem fixed and stable?	• Generally positive, depending on the competing technologies and qualification requirements. • If the design is in flux, the ability to change the design without having to redesign and remake tooling is an advantage.
Desired Production Quantities, Rate, and Time Span	• How many identical parts are needed and over what time period?	• Generally negative for high quantities and rates. • AM is generally not considered high-volume compared to injection molding, stamping, etc., so each part has a cross-over point where AM is not desirable.
Lead Time for 1st and Subsequent Parts	• How quickly do I need my first part? • How quickly do I need the rest of the parts?	• Varies directly with the answer and the qualification requirements. • AM can generally produce a first part very quickly, and depending on the rate, may be able to complete the run more quickly than processes that require tooling and assembly.
Cost to Produce 1st and Subsequent Parts	• How much does the first part, including qualification costs, cost? • How much do subsequent parts cost?	• Varies directly with the answer and the qualification requirements. • Cross-over point with higher-volume processes.
Need for Part Replacement or Repair	• Will the part require replacement or repair in the future? • How many years from the end of production will replacement and repair be needed?	• Very unsettled at the moment. • AM processes, since they are less tooling-dependent are potentially better for low-volume spares and repairs. • Evolving nature of technology means that machines and processes for replacement parts may be obsoleted more frequently.

a physical part to illustrate advanced design concepts with complex surfaces (Figure 9). They then moved to low-speed wind tunnel and physical models to validate fit-up and assembly sequences. The desire for high-speed wind tunnel models in aerospace, with higher stresses and temperatures, meant a transition to processes with higher property polymers, and ultimately to metals. At this point, AM is the dominant method for physically demonstrating concepts and making functional prototypes.

The transition of AM to actual prototype systems in the aerospace and automotive industries has been the subject of hundreds of presentations. However, this transition required the implemented AM processes to successfully address feasibility and desirability:

- **Feasibility** - The AM parts needed to be actual size versus the generally subscale requirements for wind tunnel models and concept demonstrations. Additionally, the parts need to carry service loads, albeit for reduced lifetimes or below ultimate stresses.
- **Performance Impact** - In many cases, the purpose of prototyping is to demonstrate or trade

FIGURE 9. **Potential of material extrusion to illustrate a complex design concept.**

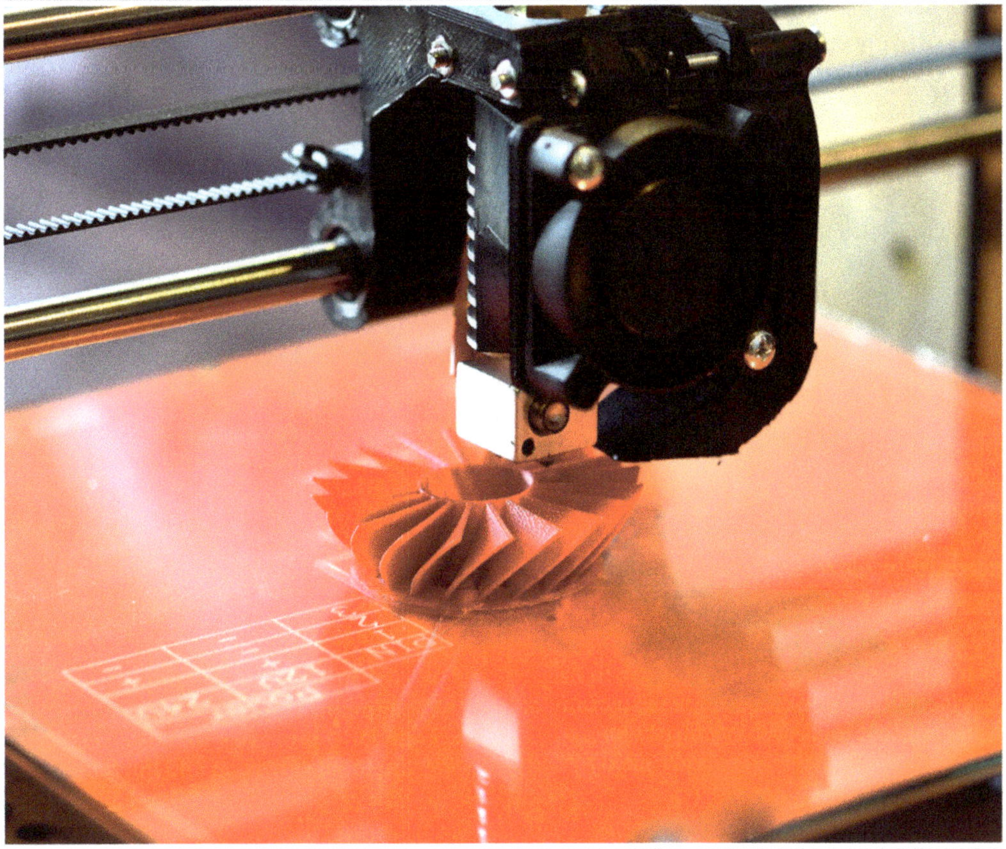

MarinaGrigorivna/Shutterstock.com.

performance, where AM's ability to rapidly change configuration can help optimize performance.

- **Design Stability** - This illustrates the advantage of AM in that different configurations can be tried rapidly.
- **Quantities** - Prototypes tend to be in small quantities; hence, the lower production rate of AM is not an issue.
- **Lead Time and Cost** - The lack of tooling to produce and the ability to unitize an AM part is an advantage in rapidly prototyping a system, subsystem, or subassembly.
- **Replacement Need** - The short service lives of prototype parts generally mean that replacements are not needed.

Because of the success in the use of AM for concepts and lightly stressed parts in the mobility industry, the challenges in the future primarily reside in applying the technology to prototypes with higher service requirements:

- High temperatures, pressures, and extended test lives in gasoline, diesel, turbine, and rocket engines
- Critical parts in flight-test and early production airframes and subsystems, where damage tolerance requirements still need to be demonstrated for flight approval
- Crash and impact driven parts in automotive, where it will be necessary to show equivalence to mass-produced parts and assemblies

Recommendations Work currently being done to extend the use of AM to production engines, airframes, and subsystems will, in large part, address the challenges for the first two cases. One thing that would be beneficial, however, is adapt NDT and damage-tolerance analysis methods to better integrate assumptions of discontinuities in prototype parts with their impact on short service life parts. In the third case, a combination of analytical modeling and validation testing will be needed in order to demonstrate the ability to predict the crash equivalence of slightly different geometries.

Quicker and Lower Cost Tooling and Safety Devices

Progress and Unresolved Issues Like concepts and prototypes, AM is often the first choice for tooling and safety devices due to the ability to go directly from CAD to part, and because each one is often a single unique piece. Material extrusion and laser PBF polymers are the dominant process and material combinations for safety devices, drill templates, assembly fixtures (shown in Figure 10), and check fixtures. While DED and laser PBF have made some inroads into injection molding dies with conforming cooling channels, the advent of low-cost metal material extrusion and binder jetting processes is moving AM to more applications, such as forming dies and robotic end effectors.

AM has successfully addressed feasibility and desirability for tooling and safety devices:

- **Feasibility** - While initial applications were limited by machine size, the continuous growth in machines, especially in polymer material extrusion machines, means that tools over five meters long are being produced. Since many tools are sized by stiffness and geometry, good design and the use of local metal reinforcements can result in a tool that meets mechanical property requirements.
- **Performance Impact** - The use of conformal cooling in injection molding dies enables them to perform longer and with a shorter time between shots.
- **Design Stability, Quantities, and Lead Time** - Since many tools and safety devices are one of a kind, AM supports rapid design and build. Additionally, the use of parametric modeling techniques means that a new tool can be automatically designed if a part's configuration changes.
- **Cost** - The ability to build directly from a CAD model and bypass intermediate steps often results in cost savings.
- **Replacement Need** - The need for replacement parts is often unpredictable, as it is often due to inadvertent damage or design changes. Thus the ability of AM to quickly produce replacement parts from a digital file is advantageous.

While AM is broadly used in the tooling and safety device domains, challenges to further applications include

- Size limitations in highly stressed tools, such as stamping and forging dies due to residual stresses in DED processes, and dimensional accuracy in material extrusion and binder jetting processes

FIGURE 10. Assembly fixture (Image courtesy: MAHLE and Stratasys Direct).

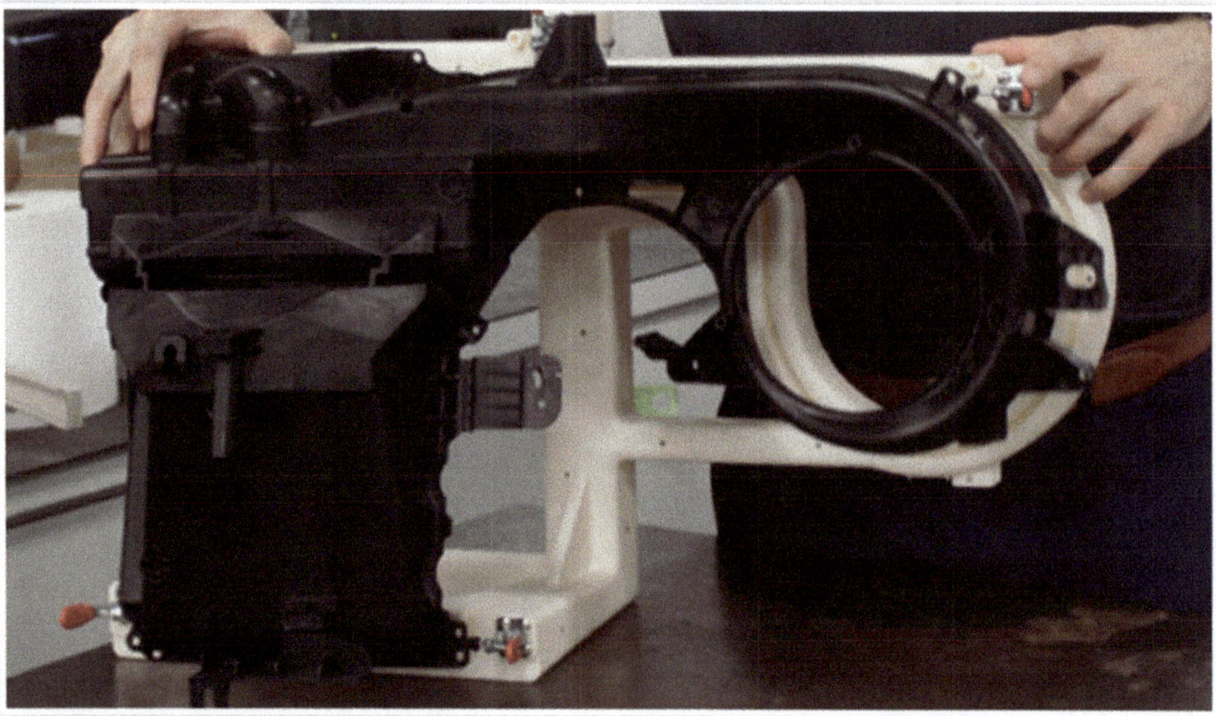

- Stiffness in larger polymer tools
- Environmental stability in polymer tools

Recommendations Moving to larger sizes in DED tools will require a combination of improved design and analysis to minimize the amount of actual deposit in the tool. This not only includes making good use of standard wrought plate but also in calculating the stresses in the tool to minimize the overall mass needed. Additionally, DED processes that reduce to overall heat input, such as melting a bare minimum of the substrate, will help. Improved dimensional accuracy in material extrusion and binder jet tools will come from developing better shrinkage predictions, on the order of what the investment casting and metal injection molding industries have achieved, as well as being able to control slumping in sections that are not solid.

The use of particulate and short fiber-reinforced feedstock will not only improve the stiffness of polymer tools but will also lower the coefficient of thermal expansion and moisture pick-up. Another potential solution to environmental stability is the use of coatings to seal the tool from the atmosphere.

Short-Run Spares, Repairs, and Hard-to-Obtain/Retain Skills

Progress and Unresolved Issues While AM has been widely touted as a solution for spares, repairs, and hard-to-obtain/retain skills, it has not yet had the hoped-for impact in the mobility industry, with the exception of lightly loaded, nonstructural parts in aircraft and rail interiors. The primary obstacle to implementation is that in the mobility industry, qualifying and certifying a spare part or repair, even for a limited lifetime, is often nearly as rigorous and time consuming as a full-life production part. Additionally, there are many fewer units produced to justify the time and cost required for qualification and certification. Something as simple as a "bathtub fitting" (Figure 11), which is used to locally reinforce structure in aging aircraft, often needs to carry the expected load for many hundreds or thousands of hours. As a result, the process and product must be carefully developed and qualified, which is much more difficult than designing a machined fitting from plate stock.

Repairs using conventional technology often have significant nonrecurring activities (e.g., tooling, process development, and qualification, especially for weld repairs) that need to be taken into consideration when determining the use of AM for spares as well. It also needs to be considered that even if limited-life spares are allowed, the product lifecycle management systems need to be able to reliably flag the part for removal at a time that is both safe and operationally convenient.

The challenge in the area of hard-to-obtain/retain skills, such as precision welding, is that those skills are used on very few parts, so the justification to design for AM and develop and qualify an AM process to replace those skills is difficult to make until a new product comes along that can be designed for AM.

AM is still challenged in both feasibility and desirability for spares, repairs, and hard-to-obtain/retain skills:

- **Feasibility** - Recent progress in development and qualification of production parts has generally removed this as a barrier, which includes

FIGURE 11. Bathtub fitting.

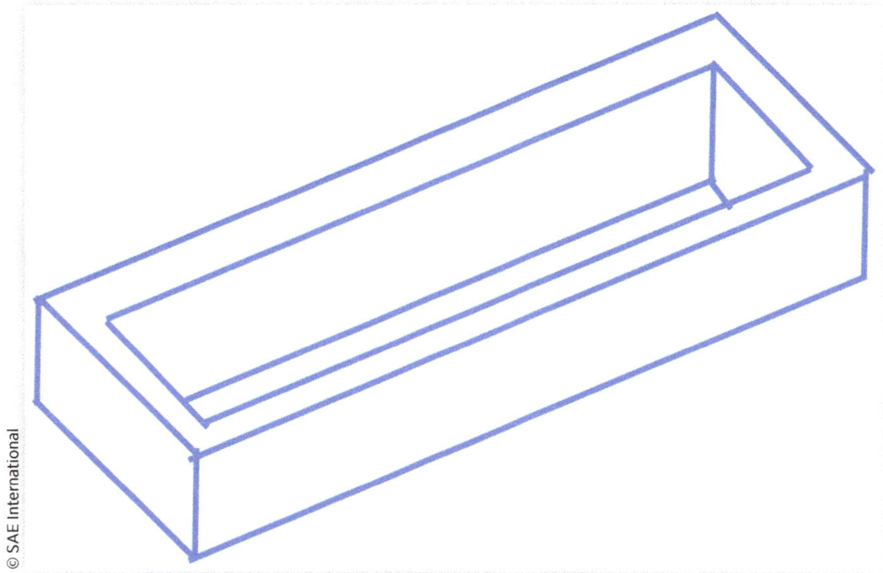

demonstrating the ability of AM to produce parts with fewer defects than welding. This is especially important in the case of repairs, where the ability to remove a larger section of part and rebuild using DED is often more predictable, and requires less operator skill than a weld repair.

- **Performance Impact** - This is rarely a criterion for these applications, provided part requirements are met.
- **Design Stability and Quantities** - The low quantities and short production span in this area takes advantage of the attributes of AM, provided lead time and cost are acceptable.
- **Lead Time** - The additional time to design, develop, and qualify an AM spare or repair often exceeds the savings of direct manufacture over conventional processes. One exception to this is for long-lead material or product form such as large die forgings or castings.
- **Cost** - Nonrecurring development, qualification, and certification costs can often make AM economically uncompetitive, unless the system can be brought back into service more quickly and there is a basis for calculating that advantage.
- **Replacement Need** - The need for replacement parts is often unpredictable, as it is often due to inadvertent damage or design changes. Thus the ability of AM to quickly produce replacement parts from a digital file is advantageous. On the other hand, this can be especially pertinent when considering a new design, where having the original part made using AM better positions one to make spares from AM.

The primary challenge for AM to become widely used for spares, repairs, and difficult skills is the cost and time for part-specific process development, qualification, and certification.

Recommendations Overcoming the primary challenge for spares, repairs, and difficult skills will require advances in the following areas

- Leveraging the understanding of the relationships between materials, input, and result in AM being developed for production hardware. In this case, the understandings already being developed can be directly applied.
- Develop methodologies to allow for the qualification and certification of spare parts that do not need to last the full life of the system. This can include things such as better fatigue crack initiation and growth methodologies.
- Organizations and industries looking to use AM to replace hard-to-obtain/retain skills need to create a 5- to 10-year roadmap of process and product development to ensure timely availability for implementation.
- Update life-management systems to ensure timely removal of limited-life parts.
- Ways to better calculate the benefits of earlier return to service in areas where those analyses do not exist.
- If the need for spares is infrequent, such as a single buy for the next five years, it makes sense to customize the requirements for qualification such that it only applies for a short spare-part run on a single machine.

Cost Reduction

Progress and Unresolved Issues The primary means of cost reduction for AM are

- Reducing material consumption and processing time for costly, difficult-to-process metals like titanium and nickel-based alloys
- Unitizing parts and reducing assembly, inventory, handling, and engineering costs
- Reducing or eliminating nonrecurring tooling costs

Tooling costs were addressed earlier, while unitization will be discussed in the section on part-count reduction. The use of DED processes to reduce titanium and nickel-based part costs in aircraft has been widely reported and shows feasibility, although the number of published implementations at this moment number in the tens rather than the hundreds or thousands which the AM industry certainly hopes for. These parts are generally 100% machined, so the finished part is often identical as would be obtained from a wrought product form. The primary challenges to date are

- Cost of feedstock and AM machine time, which is more costly on a unit basis, even though the preform is significantly smaller than a plate or die forging. Residual stress management and control also significantly increase process time and steps for larger parts.
- Cost of quality assurance, such as NDT and witness coupon testing, which is much higher on a unit basis than for bulk products like plate and bar.
- The aerospace industry is taking a phased, deliberate approach to ensure successful initial implementations, while preparing the ground for widespread use. This means that larger, more critical parts that have lower unit costs for quality assurance, and more dramatic material and machining savings have yet to be implemented. This also means that the time and cost for qualification

whittles away at savings from eliminating tooling versus conventional technology.

- Continuous improvement in machining technology, which will be discussed later in this report.

Recommendations The challenge of the deliberate approach taken by the aerospace industry is being addressed with each implementation. As more is understood of the material/processing/property relationships and confidence in the process is gained, the application space, especially in parts driven by durability and damage tolerance, will continue to grow. Higher confidence in the process will also allow witness coupon testing to be performed once for a lot of multiple parts versus for each part. Better prediction and management of residual stresses are needed to enable higher build rates, nearer-net shapes, and larger parts, which will further reduce costs. Finally, advances in automated ultrasonic inspection and interpretation of complex part geometries are necessary to not only address NDT costs, but also to reduce intermediate machining for inspectability and improved reliability of discontinuity detection.

Mass Customization

Progress and Unresolved Issues In general, the mobility industry has not taken advantage of AM's potential for mass customization, as it can be considered the antithesis of what the industry has been striving for over the last century:

- Stable and repeatable processes and products for safety and performance, even something as mundane as customized environmental system controls in an automobile, could have crash-safety implications.
- Commonality to reduce changeover costs and deliver a consistent customer experience.

As a result, the mobility industry is still looking for a benefit from mass customization, outside the niche markets of customized automobiles and private jet interiors, with customization also being seen in the rail sector. One innovative use of mass customization, implemented in the Reichsbahn stations in Germany, used laser PBF to make thousands of unique Braille plaques to help visually impaired travelers navigate through the stations.

Recommendations Unlike the medical industry, the mobility industry has not generally needed mass customization. A potential area where mid-customization could apply would be in aircraft or passenger railcar interiors, where an operator could have commonality in its interiors, regardless of the original manufacturer. This could not only give an operator a signature appearance but could potentially reduce its inventory of spare parts.

Part-Count Reduction

Progress and Unresolved Issues In discussing part-count reduction, it needs to be recognized that it is the means to an end, as opposed to an end in itself. Part-count reduction must provide some benefit to the user:

- Higher performance, by reducing fasteners with their stress concentrations, discontinuous load paths, and duplicative overlapping structure; higher performance can also be achieved by reducing drag for fluid flow passages.
- Higher reliability by reducing stress concentrations and opportunities for crevice corrosion.
- Lower costs by reducing assembly operations, assembly fixtures, part tracking, and the engineering costs associated with more parts.

When part reduction is applied correctly, costs and times can be dramatically decreased and performance significantly improved (Figure 12). When applied incorrectly, part-count reduction can result in larger, more expensive parts that need to be completely replaced or expensively repaired for minor manufacturing or in-service wear or damage. It can also result in attempts to produce parts of size or complexity outside the capability of a given process. Specific to AM, the following issues can arise when reducing part count:

- The ability of the part to undergo NDT to the desired level of sensitivity and reliability is compromised.
- Access to surfaces that need to be treated or inspected is eliminated, or other post-processing can be made more difficult.
- Thermal distortion in metal parts either during build or post-processing can result in excessive rework or scrappage.
- Build times may become so long that they approach the mean time between failure for the AM machine.

Recommendations Because the benefits and drawbacks to part-count reduction are generally not unique to AM, the primary recommendation is that organizations transitioning to AM ensure that their DfAM training includes what needs to be considered when using AM to reduce part count, including reasonable build time.

Performance Improvements

Progress and Unresolved Issues Nearly every month brings news of AM resulting in some form of performance improvement in the aerospace industry. As AM costs decrease, this trend will move to the rail and automotive sectors. In the case of aerospace, the vast majority of announcements are related to improved efficiency and reliability. In addition to Figure 12, another example of this is a heat exchanger made

FIGURE 12. **GE catalyst turboprop engine (Image courtesy: GE Additive).**

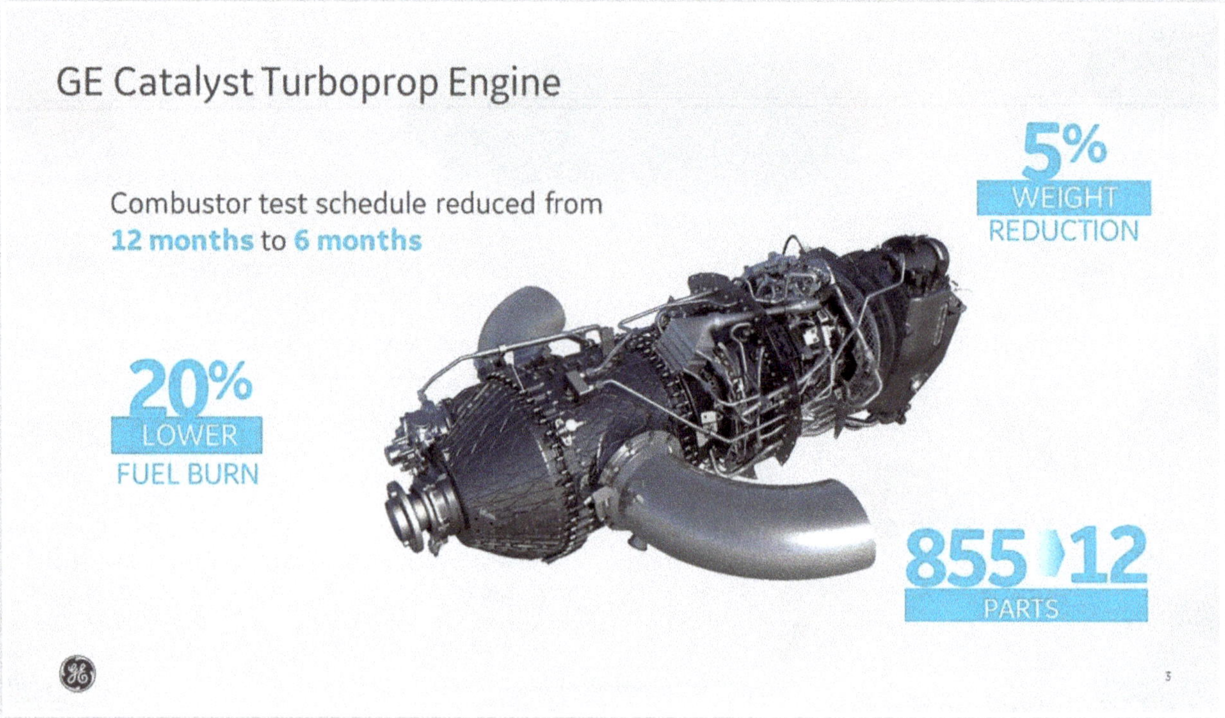

using sheet lamination that is significantly more efficient that the baseline brazed design (Figure 13).

While these implementations are documenting success, the primary obstacles to broader performance improvements are

- **Surface roughness in metal parts** - While this will be discussed in a future SAE EDGE™ Research Report, surface finish impacts the potential performance gains from AM in a variety of ways. In structural parts, the reduced fatigue performance can more than eliminate the efficiency gains from an AM-enabled design. In fluid-flow parts, the roughness can increase pressure drop and eliminate the performance gains from optimized-flow paths.
- **Analytical techniques** - Many of the current certified analytical techniques were developed around conventional manufacturing. In the case of aircraft, it was sheet metal buildup. Transition to unitized high-speed machined parts in the 1990s required a revision, even though the geometry changes were relatively minor compared to the potential transformation to AM.
- **Uncertainty in the sources of variability and defects** - The relationships between process and performance are not as well understood for wrought products. While both AM and wrought metallic processing have in excess of 100 parameters as they are, the latter has a two-century head start regarding modern research. Not only are the absolute and relative impacts of those parameters and their interactions on microstructure, properties, and defects much better understood, but wrought material has a long history that provides a statistical basis of confidence as well.
- **An understanding in the engineering community of the potential for performance improvement that AM brings** - This includes the engineering team having the ability, software tools, and process understanding to create advantageous designs for AM.

Recommendations The recommendations to overcome the barriers to performance are the inverse of the barriers, namely, improvements in surface roughness, analytical techniques, better understanding of process-performance relationships, and expansion of DfAM (both the benefits and limitations) in organizations adopting AM.

FIGURE 13. Heat exchanger.

Reprinted with permission from Fabrisonic

Trade-offs in Product Design, Development, and Deployment

Trade Space in an Evolving Technology Area

The unique factor in working with an evolving technology is that the trade space continually changes with time - both the time to make the decision and the time when the technology needs to be deployed. Therefore, the typical trade space elements of nonrecurring cost, recurring cost, lead time, risk, and performance have additional considerations, along with considerations of design flexibility.

Nonrecurring Cost

While AM shares most of the nonrecurring costs of conventional manufacturing technologies such as design, analysis, programming, and supplier and part qualification, the following nonrecurring costs are different with AM. This is also where part-count reduction shines, as the engineering, programming, and tooling for a part or assembly that is not needed is free:

- **Development and Acquisition of AM Skills** - Successful implementation of AM requires a team that is skilled in disciplines including part requirements and design, DfAM, AM materials and processes, AM machine operation, post-processing, and even supply chain management and contracting. Not only do the team members need to develop their own skills but they need to learn to delegate to the other members, especially if those skills reside in another organization or company. The end result is that for the initial applications, the development and acquisition of these skills will represent a significant nonrecurring cost.
- **Design and Analysis** - Most organizations and designers will go through a learning curve to properly design and analyze AM parts (except for identical replacements), so initial implementations will be a bit more costly. This can also include the

need to develop new design, analysis, qualification, and certification processes and tools.

- **Programming** - Build programs for AM parts generally take less time than numerically controlled machining programs, and the tools are getting continually better with time. Since many AM parts require interface machining, there will still be some numeric control programming cost.
- **Tooling** - This is another area where AM generally provides a benefit, noting that many parts machined from plate often do not require tools and that some metal AM parts may require heat-treatment fixtures, while metal material extrusion and binder jetting can require setters for sintering.
- **Process Development** - The first implementation in an organization can require months of process development, along with the development of design values. In much of the mobility industry to date, this is treated as an enterprise investment versus a nonrecurring cost for the first implementation. That said, process development for a single part can still require several months and multiple iterations. This is a cost that will drop quickly as an organization gains experience. Note that other technologies, such as machined from plate, casting, and forging can also require multiple iterations as well (with this cost usually rolled up into a few nonrecurring line items in a proposal).
- **Qualification** - Parts and industries with stringent qualification requirements often have qualification costs that are many times that for conventional technologies, especially for parts with safety impacts. As an organization gains experience in AM, these costs will approach that of conventional technologies, provided the design space for the AM process is not expanding as well.

Recurring Cost

Recurring cost in AM primarily differs from conventional manufacturing in two ways:

- **Facility Utilization** - Since many organizations and service bureaus are adding capacity and staff in preparation for the future, their AM machines or post-processing facilities may be underutilized or overstaffed. This is often exasperated by having excess capacity to reduce production volume ramp-up risk due to the longer process times for many AM processes. When doing a recurring cost comparison, it is important to consider what the cost will be at later points in the production run as utilization increases.
- **Scrap and Rework** - With the exception of polymer prototypes, tooling, and safety devices, many AM facilities do not have a long-enough history of the cost of scrap, rework, and its impact on delivered part cost. This is further complicated in that engineering organizations are regularly pushing the boundaries of AM technology. Therefore, when performing a cost-benefit analysis for using AM, it is important to consider how the part maker is calculating the cost of scrap and rework, as the calculation can go either way, depending on their business risk.

Lead Time

There are two main points one needs to consider regarding lead time:

- **Process Development and Qualification** - These generally take longer for a new AM part than conventional manufacturing, with the difference growing shorter on subsequent implementations, while tooling and programming costs are generally shorter for AM. As an organization matures in its implementation of an AM technology, the lead time benefit will shift to AM, just as it did in the mature applications of prototypes and tooling.
- **Concurrency** - Depending on both the AM and its competing manufacturing technology, different combinations of concurrency in design, programming, tooling, build, qualify, and produce for either technology will produce different results. Therefore, the organization must decide on levels of concurrency that are consistent with their risk analysis.

Risk

As with any manufacturing process, a decision to pursue AM carries performance, schedule, and cost risks. The key decision in an AM risk analysis is whether or not to carry a conventional manufacturing backup, how the design and cost of the backup differs, and at what point does one decide to drop the backup and concentrate resources on the AM solution.

Performance

The wide range of successful AM applications, where weight has been saved or thermal performance has been improved in spite of lower mechanical or thermal properties, has demonstrated the ability of good DfAM to compensate for these when used in the correct applications. The main barrier to this in structural metal parts is the impact of surface roughness on fatigue properties. Thus the primary trade-off in deciding to use AM to make a part is whether or not adding an additional 5% or 10% margin in the most highly stressed zones adds enough weight, thermal resistance, or cost to make the payoff not worthwhile. Accordingly, the pass/fail criteria for the witness coupons can be reduced by that additional margin, with the use of statistical process control to ensure process stability. As an organization gains more experience and statistical data, that additional margin can be reduced.

One of the more exciting areas in metal AM is the design and development of alloys for AM processes. Almost all of the alloys used today in AM were developed for wrought or cast products, meaning they are not optimized for the unique circumstances present in metal AM. As the design and development of these alloys bear fruit in the next decade, a point will be reached where an AM part could actually have superior mechanical properties to a wrought or cast design.

Design Flexibility

While some designs in the mobility industry are released and never changed throughout the product life cycle, others receive planned or unplanned revisions. Thus the likelihood of a part design changing, along with the impact to the manufacturing operations, needs to be taken into account when making a decision to use AM. While often considered to be more amenable to design changes, if a part made using AM requires extensive qualification testing, and the conventional process would only require a minor change to a numerically controlled program, the conventional option is actually more flexible.

Recommendations

When considering AM, it is important that the combined design/development/qualification/build approach for both the AM process and the relevant competing technologies be compared in a consistent manner that also weighs the risk of either approach not meeting the intended goals. Not only does this need to consider the status at the time of initial design release but also throughout the product life cycle. Finally, when developing a long-term strategy for AM implementation, an understanding of where the processes and materials are headed will position an organization for continued success.

Competing Technologies

Nothing Is Static

While this report has frequently mentioned that AM technology is continuously changing, it also needs to be considered that conventional technologies are also continually changing, which means that while this year's solution is conventional, and next year's is AM, the year after could be conventional as well, unsettling the desirability AM for a given application.

Machining, Robotics, and Numeric Control Programming

The last 30 years have seen a revolution in machining in the mobility industry, particularly in aerospace. Advances in machine tools and machining dynamics have resulted in an order-of-magnitude decrease in machining times for aluminum alloys such that material cost is dominant for large (greater than one square meter) monolithic parts. The same improvements, along with advances in cutting tools, have reduced the time for machining titanium and nickel-based alloys to the point that machining cost generally runs slightly less than material cost. These advancements will continue to make machining more cost competitive, while advances in robotics will further reduce the tooling and labor cost for assembly. Advancements in numeric control and robotic programming tools will continue to reduce the cost and schedule time for these nonrecurring operations in both machined parts and assemblies. An emerging trend in machined parts has been tighter tolerances, including the drilling of high-tolerance holes on the machine tool, as opposed to drill on assembly. This raises the chinning bar for AM parts in terms of performance and cost. Finally, robotics and numeric control technologies have been combined in a technology known as incremental sheet metal forming, which either completely or significantly eliminates the need for tooling in making sheet metal parts (Figure 14).

Indirect AM

Indirect AM, described earlier in this report, is also impacting conventional technology. Binder jet printing of molds and cores is already widespread in the casting industry, such that casting can cover a wider range of production quantities than ever before. Extrusion-based processes are used to make investment casting patterns that are the equivalent of those from injection wax molds, which also closes the quantity gap in investment casting.

While the decades-long depth of understanding automotive that companies have in sheet metal forming has led people to think of it as an old technology, sheet metal forming has significant advantages in mass production due to speed of processing and efficiency of material utilization. When combined with robotics, bonding, and welding, complex unitized structures can be made. Now the use of AM to make sheet metal forming tools is also addressing the nonrecurring cost and lead time drawback of sheet metal forming.

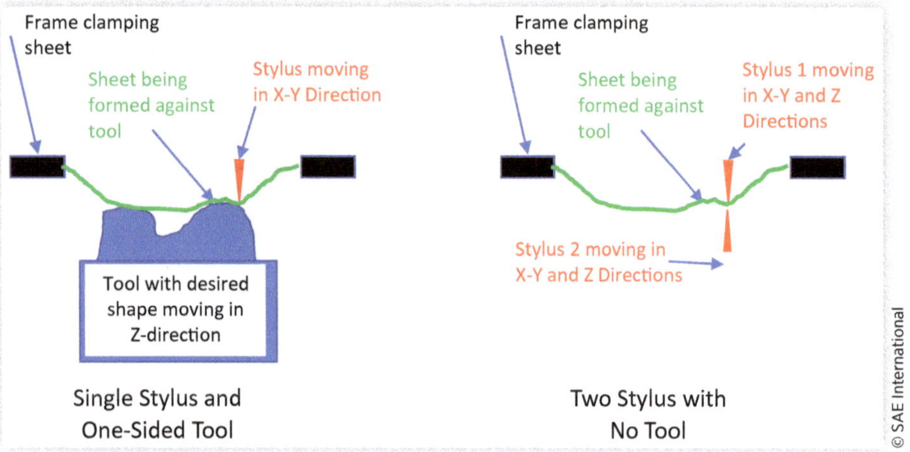

FIGURE 14. Incremental sheet forming.

The lesson to be considered is that AM is not only introducing a new way of making parts but also that AM is changing the way conventional manufacturing is making parts.

Recommendations

The primary recommendation for a team considering the use of AM is to understand that other technologies are also continually evolving.

Summary

Implementing an Unsettled Technology

Determining whether or not to implement an unsettled technology like AM requires not only the usual understanding of part requirements, process capabilities, and limitations but an appreciation of both the quantifiable and unquantifiable risks and opportunities. Also, with the exception of polymer concepts, prototypes, tooling, and safety devices, it still takes a bit of an investment mindset that the initial implementations will pave the way for more beneficial future implementations, in the same manner that fiberglass/phenolic composites and investment castings paved the way for carbon/epoxy wings and fuselages and single-crystal superalloy castings for turbines.

Checklist for Determining Feasibility and Desirability

Many organizations and teams in the mobility industry have processes, procedures, and data to support determining the feasibility and desirability of using AM for a given application. For those who are either beginning their journey or looking to determine if further expansion of their use of AM will bring them further benefit, Tables 3 and 4 provide a checklist to use as a guide, with Figure 15 providing a useful decision flow.

Product Team and Organization Recommendations

The dynamic nature of both AM and conventional technology means that the feasibility and desirability of using AM in a given mobility application will be an unsettled topic for the next 20 years, as AM technology continues to mature. Therefore, a product team or organization considering the use of AM either for a single application or to make fundamental changes in the way the design and build their mobility products should be considering the following:

- Develop a full understanding of the benefits, limitations, and trade-offs of AM for the full product life cycle, as described in this SAE EDGE™ Research Report.
- Develop an organizational strategy around what to develop internally in terms of team skills, processes, materials, and data generation, and where to leverage external sources for the same.
- Gain an understanding of DfAM for the processes of interest.
- Remember that waiting for the perfect solution can prevent you from reaping benefits in the near term and ensuring your company is around in the long term. Because AM technology is maturing quickly, if you find an AM solution that meets requirements and is cost effective today, it is better to exploit it now, knowing your organization will be better placed to exploit future advances in the technology.

TABLE 3. **Feasibility checklist.**

#	Question
F1	Are the machines available for the process of interest large enough to make the part, accounting for the necessary bulld orlentation?
F2	If the answer to the above is no, can the part be broken into smaller pieces without compromising the reason for using AM?
F3	Are there any post-processing operations that would limit part size?
F4	Can the processes of interest produce a part of the desired geometry that maintains the reason for using AM?
F5	Can the processes of interest make the part of a material that meets the service requirements?
F6	If the part/material can meet all service requirements except service life, is a shorter replacement/service interval acceptable?
F7	Is the process and material of interest sufficiently mature to deliver a part that meets service requriements in the desired timeframe?
F8	Are the mechanical properties of the process and material of interest sufficiently characterized to provide confidence of ability to meet service requirements and have an acceptable production yield?
F9	Are there any concerns that the material and process combination for the part have discontinuities that would be undetectable and comprise the ability to meet service requirements?
F10	Is there enough production capacity in place or planned to meet the desired production rate?

- Keep abreast of near-term, mid-term, and long-term trends and progress in the area of AM and conventional technology, as barriers to wider implementation, such as NDT and surface roughness, may eventually be overcome.

SAE EDGE™ Research Reports

SAE EDGE™ Research Reports, like the present report on "Unsettled Topics on the Feasibility and Desirability of Using Additive Manufacturing in the Mobility Industry," are intended to push further out into still unsettled areas of technology of interest to the mobility industry. SAE launches these reports before attempting to form a joint working group, let alone a cooperative research program or a standards committee.

SAE EDGE™ Research Reports are intended to be quick, concise overviews of major unsettled areas where vital new technologies are emerging. An unsettled area is characterized more by confusion and controversy than established order. Early practitioners must confront an absence of agreement. Their challenge is often not to seize the high ground but to find common ground. These scouting reports from the frontiers of investigation are intended merely to begin the process of sorting through critical issues, contributing to a better understanding of key problems, and providing helpful suggestions about possible next steps and avenues of investigation.

SAE EDGE™ Research Reports, therefore, are fundamentally distinct from the more formal working groups approach and far removed from the more mature research program and standard's development process.

Next Steps on the Feasibility and Desirability of Using Additive Manufacturing in the Mobility Industry

This publication should be considered only as a first step toward clarifying the issues around the feasibility and desirability of using additive manufacturing in the mobility industry. The intention behind this and other SAE EDGE™ Research Reports is to start a dialogue among interested parties on important industry-wide topics that require further attention. The expectation is that these explorations of unsettled areas of technology will lead to the formation of working groups and, ultimately,

TABLE 4. Desirability checklist.

#	Question
D1	Does the AM process and material combination result in a part or subsystem with higher performance?
D2	Can the higher performance be quantified and used to trade against negative impacts (if any) of the AM process and material combination?
D3	Do the engineering and manufacturing teams have enough familiarity with DfAM to fully exploit the capabilities of AM?
D4	Is the design of the part or subsystem fixed and stable?
D5	Could the design possibly change as a result of pre-production testing?
D6	Could the design possibly change as a result of initial service use?
D7	Could the design possibly change if sales differ widely from expectations?
D8	Could the manufacturing process change if sales differ widely from expectations?
D9	What is the production rate and volume in full production?
D10	What is the production volume between design changes?
D11	What is the total time span for production, and how will it ramp up or down?
D12	What is the lead time needed to have a conceptual prototype?
D13	What is the lead time needed to have a functioning prototype?
D14	What is the lead time needed for a test part that carries full loads, but not full lifetime?
D15	What is the lead time needed for the final production part?
D16	Does concurrency in the design, program, build, test, and qualify steps reduce lead time and an acceptable risk?
D17	For both the AM and conventional options, are all the steps, along with their cost and time for developing the production processes understood and accounted for?
D18	Are the tools and programs for all steps of the AM and conventional production processes accounted for?
D19	Are the time and cost of qualification for both the AM and conventional processes understood?
D20	If production isn't continuous, what is the lead time needed from time to order until the part needs to be available?
D21	Will the part require replacement or repair in the future?
D22	What is the expected annual volume of needed part repairs and replacements?
D23	Will part replacements take place for an extended period of time (>5 years) after production ends?
D24	Would replacing or making repairs on a part require extensive non-recurring activities (tooling, development and qualification) for a non-AM part?
D25	Can the lifecycle management systems accommodate repairs and replacement parts that are less than full life, if full life is generally expected?
D26	Will a unique repair be required for every part, or will the same repair be used repeatedly?
D27	Will facility utilization have an influence on production cost?

committees that can address and resolve the issues they raise, producing a framework for developing a common vocabulary of definitions, best practices, protocols, and standards needed to support continued progress toward safer and more innovative automotive products.

This SAE EDGE™ Research Report on AM identifies the following key topics for further pursuit, both through continued informal discussions among industry practitioners and through more formal working groups:

- Extend the current plan for public specifications to cover a wider range of material and process combinations, and have those specifications include statistically derived minimum properties.
- Develop public databases and materials handbooks. These would be tied to the above specifications and be akin to the old Aerospace Materials Handbooks or the Aluminum Association Handbooks. While they would not extend to the level of the Metallic Materials Properties Development and Standardization in terms of design use, they would provide a broad range of organizations with the properties they can expect to aid in material and process selection.
- Develop a standard curriculum along with common certificate and degree requirements for AM technicians and engineers, especially in the area of DfAM.

FIGURE 15. **Decision flow (reprinted with permission from Ref. [1]).**

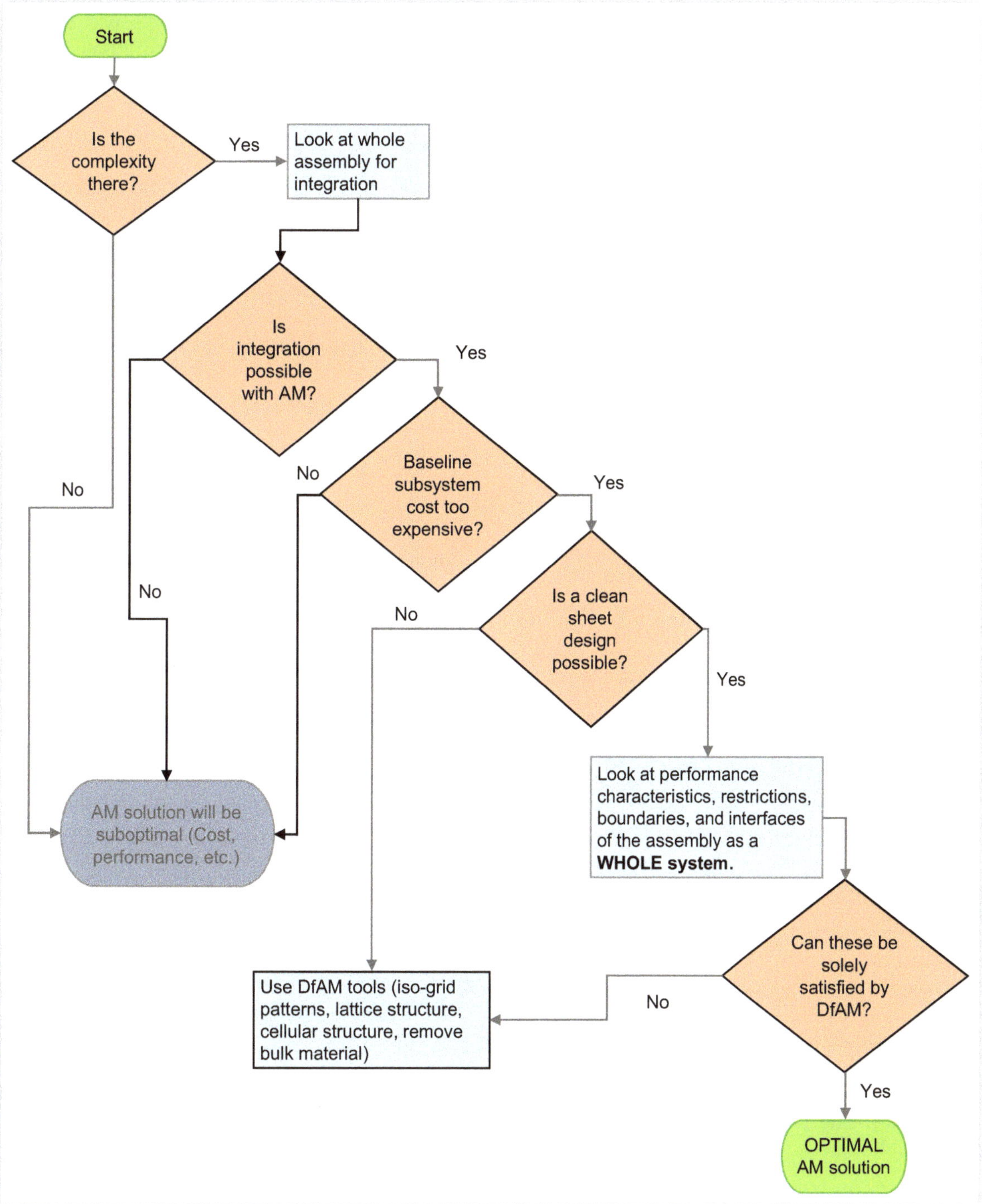

Industry Recommendations

The overall recommendations of this SAE EDGE™ Research Report can be summarized as follows:

1. Develop feature-based costing tools for AM parts that allow the user to customize for the cost structure and production rate for the application being considered. This would include methods to monetize the value of obtaining prototypes, tools, and parts more rapidly.
2. Research the characterization and impact of AM-unique surface roughness on part performance. This will create the basis for determining the needed technologies and extent of surface roughness reduction needed for a range of different materials, processes, and applications.
3. Research the impact of small, randomly distributed discontinuities on the fatigue and impact performance of a part. Since the majority of AM processes use solidification or sintering, small physical discontinuities will almost always be present. At some point, the size, distribution, and location of these transition from not impacting properties to having a significant decrement. A better understanding of this transition, combined with probabilistic methods, would enable organizations to develop ways of determining reliability for more critical AM parts.
4. Develop a tool that would help a product team rapidly trade requirements, materials, and processes to quickly narrow them down for more detailed studies.

Acronyms

3D - Three-dimensional
AM - Additive manufacturing
BR&T - Boeing Research and Technology
CAD - Computer-aided design
DED - Directed-energy deposition
DfAM - Design for additive manufacturing
NDT - Nondestructive testing
PBF - Powder bed fusion

Acknowledgments

Recognition should go first to all the participants, many of who also provided feedback on the draft version of this publication. Without their input and initiative, this SAE EDGE™ Research Report would not have been possible.

Christopher Aldridge, *The Barnes Group Advisors*
David Dietrich, PhD, *Honeywell*
Jerry Halley, *Tech Manufacturing*
Ron Daul, *General Motors*
Anthony Rollett, PhD, *Carnegie Mellon University*
Jennifer Coyne, *Wabtec*

Additional thanks go to the following individuals who also had the opportunity to provide feedback on the draft version of this publication. Their contributions helped shape this publication.

John Barnes, *The Barnes Group Advisors*

The authors of this document together with the SAE Team responsible for its creation join in expressing our deepest appreciation to all the individuals mentioned above.

Kevin T. Slattery, DSc
The Barnes Group Advisors

References

1. Dietrich, D.M., Kenworthy, M., and Cudney, E.A. *Additive Manufacturing Change Management: Best Practices (Continuous Improvement Series)* (Boca Raton: CRC Press, 2019), ISBN-13: 978-1138611757.

Contact Information

EDGEresearch@sae.org.

The authors of this document together with the SAE Team responsible for its creation join in expressing our deepest appreciation to all of the individuals who contributed.

www.ingramcontent.com/pod-product-compliance
Lightning Source LLC
LaVergne TN
LVHW070912210926
848482LV00017B/1060
* 9 7 8 1 4 6 8 6 0 1 7 1 8 *